Prefunding Social Security Benefits to Achieve Intergenerational Fairness: Can It Be Done in the Social Security Trust Fund?

Randall P. Mariger*
Staff Economist
U.S. Department of Treasury, Office of Economic Policy
Washington, DC 20551
December 2008

Prefunding Social Security Benefits to Achieve Intergenerational Fairness: Can It Be Done in the Social Security Trust Fund?

Randall P. Mariger*
Staff Economist
U.S. Department of Treasury, Office of Economic Policy
Washington, DC 20551
December 2008

Abstract

Being fair to future generations requires that Social Security be reformed in a manner that prefunds a significant share of future Social Security benefit payments. All serious reform plans have this property. Prefunding is done exclusively in the Social Security trust fund in some plans, and it is done partly in personal retirement accounts (PRAs) in others.

The consequences of prefunding Social Security in the trust fund are controversial and not well understood. The key question is whether Social Security surpluses are offset by smaller non-Social Security surpluses; if they are, and if the offset is 100 percent, then Social Security surpluses are not truly saved and prefunding intended to make Social Security fair to future generations is neutralized by a non-Social Security fiscal policy that is less fair to future generations. This paper makes this important point concrete by simulating the response of non-Social Security fiscal policy to two alternative Social Security reforms that differ only with regard to the breakdown of prefunding in the trust fund and prefunding in PRAs. The reforms simulated are the Nonpartisan Reform Plan proposed by Jeffrey Liebman, Maya McGuineas, and Andrew Samwick, and a version of that plan that prefunds exclusively in the trust fund. If Social Security surpluses are not saved, it is found that NRP's PRAs increase the net benefits of government to future generations by about 0.6 percent of GDP; that is, future generations enjoy some combination of lower non-Social Security taxes and higher non-Social Security government spending that amounts to about 0.6 percent of GDP in every year.

The paper also reviews budget politics over the past 30 years and concludes that there is a substantial probability that trust fund accumulations are largely offset by reduced non-Social Security surpluses.

The implications of these findings for Social Security reform are explored. If budget politics precludes the possibility that Social Security surpluses are saved, then large dividends would be paid if an alternative means of effectively prefunding Social Security could be found. If politics also precludes that possibility, then it would be rational to compromise other Social Security reform objectives so as to reduce trust fund accumulations. Specifically, relative to a first-best reform with effective prefunding, smaller benefit levels would be appropriate.

---

*The analysis and conclusions set forth in this paper are those of the author and do not indicate concurrence by other members of the Treasury research staff or Treasury's senior officials.

I. Introduction

Being fair to future generations requires that Social Security be reformed in a manner that prefunds a significant share of future Social Security benefit payments. All serious reform plans have this property. Prefunding is done exclusively in the Social Security trust fund in some plans, and it is done partly in personal retirement accounts (PRAs) in others.

A lot of confusion has arisen in recent years over whether Social Security trust fund accumulations represent real saving. On one side of the debate it is argued that trust fund accumulations do not represent real saving because they are comprised of special-issue government securities–government IOUs to itself. A prominent example of this view of the trust funds is contained in Congressional testimony given by the Congressional Budget Office's Director and Deputy Director in February 1999:

> "…the federal government's trust funds are not trust funds in the traditional sense; that is, they do not set aside current income for future use. …..But the Treasury securities held by federal trust funds are nothing more than the government's IOUs to itself. Look at it this way: if the government had truly invested trust fund net income for future use, the Treasury would currently be holding hundreds of billions of dollars of real assets that could be liquidated in the future to pay for future obligations. But the Treasury does not hold any net assets; in fact, all that remains from the so-called investment of trust fund surpluses is net debt to the public of $3.7 trillion. ….. Nor does it [the trust fund] affect the government's ability to pay those benefits."[1]

A narrow interpretation of this statement is true: Because the trust fund is not a claim on third parties, somehow losing the trust fund information would have no effect on the government's ability to finance its operations going forward. However, the statement strongly implies an untruth that many find credible and take to be its point: That it is impossible for the government to set aside income for future use if the income is invested in "IOUs to itself" and trust fund accumulations therefore cannot under any circumstances increase the government's capacity to pay future Social Security benefits.

Advocates of prefunding Social Security in the trust fund make equally deceptive arguments. Many argue that the trust fund is real simply because a positive balance conveys the legislative authority to pay Social Security benefits, and dismiss the question of whether those balances represent real wealth as irrelevant. Others explicitly acknowledge a likelihood that the trust fund does not represent real wealth, and seem to view that as a problem, but they nevertheless advocate policies that would rely on trust fund accumulations to make Social Security solvent. For example, Bill Novelli, the President of AARP, writes:

> "By 2040, the trust fund will have run through its "stored up" assets and will depend entirely on the incoming payroll taxes from the smaller pool of workers at that time. The

---

[1] Congressional Budget Office (1999). This example and several others are cited in President's Commission to Strengthen Social Security (2001).

problem is made even worse because the trust fund assets aren't actually "stored up." The Treasury bonds are there alright, backed by the full faith and promise of the U.S. government. But the actual money itself is borrowed and spent each year as part of the general budget. If instead, the money were used to pay down national debt, it would make the government borrowing cheaper when the time comes to pay out interest and principal on the Social Security bonds. Alarmists picture this scenario as bankruptcy for Social Security. It isn't. ..... The system has enough money to pay benefits at current rates until 2040. ..... And if our elected officials act reasonably soon, full funding could be restored with a relatively small increase in the payroll tax, a reduction in benefits, or some mixture of both."[2]

It is acknowledged that the "problem is made worse" because the trust fund is not truly saved, but nevertheless the policies advocated—payroll tax increases, benefit cuts, or both—are ones that make the system solvent largely by increasing trust fund accumulations.

As serious observers of fiscal policy are aware, the issue is not how the trust fund is invested or whether a positive trust fund balance conveys legislative authority to pay benefits, but whether Social Security surpluses pay down debt held by the public. (Novelli alludes to this in the above quote but seems not to appreciate the implications.) If Social Security policy does not influence non-Social Security policy, then the trust fund balance at every date represents the amount by which past Social Security cash flows have reduced debt held by the public at that time. Reducing a liability in this manner is real saving that increases the government's capacity to pay future Social Security benefits. In this case, the trust fund measures real wealth put aside to pay future Social Security benefits and reforms that rely on trust fund accumulations to make Social Security nominally solvent also make it truly solvent.

On the other hand, many analysts believe that Social Security surpluses are offset all or in part by lower non-Social Security surpluses. If the offset is 100 percent, then Social Security surpluses do not increase the government's capacity to pay future Social Security benefits. In this case, the trust fund is not a real store of value and reforms that rely on trust fund accumulations to make Social Security solvent do so at the expense of a less solvent non-Social Security policy. Because the policy fails to improve the overall fiscal balance, this paper refers to such policies as being nominally solvent but not truly solvent.

This paper makes these important points formally and illustrates the importance of the distinction between nominal and true solvency by simulating the response of non-Social Security fiscal policy to two alternative Social Security reforms that differ only with regard to the breakdown of prefunding in the trust fund and prefunding in PRAs. The reforms simulated are the Nonpartisan Reform Plan (NRP) proposed in Liebman, McGuineas, and Samwick (2005), and a version of that plan that prefunds exclusively in the trust fund. If Social Security surpluses are not saved, it is found that NRP's PRAs increase the net benefits of government to future generations by about 0.6 percent of

---

[2] Novelli and Workman (2006), p. 197.

GDP; that is, future generations enjoy some combination of lower non-Social Security taxes and higher non-Social Security government spending that amounts to about 0.6 percent of GDP in every year.

The paper also reviews budget politics over the past 30 years and concludes that there is a substantial probability that trust fund accumulations are largely offset by reduced non-Social Security surpluses.

Lastly, the paper considers the implications for policy of being constrained to attempt prefunding in the trust fund when such prefunding is offset with smaller non-Social Security surpluses. It is concluded that relative to a first-best reform with effective prefunding, a second-best policy with ineffective prefunding calls for lower benefits levels.

Before proceeding, the terms "nominal solvency" and "true solvency" merit further clarification. A Social Security policy that is projected to result in a positive trust fund balance into perpetuity but which *causes* lower non-Social Security surpluses is referred to as nominally solvent and not truly solvent. With a nominally solvent Social Security system, the non-Social Security budget would be stressed at such time as the Social Security system draws on trust fund accumulations to pay benefits. How fiscal policy should adapt in those circumstances is beyond the scope of the paper. In particular, it is not suggested that all or some of the adaptations should be in the Social Security budget. Indeed, the paper's simulations assume that all of the adaptations are in the non-Social Security budget. The important point is that no matter how overall fiscal policy adapts, future generations suffer if Social Security accumulations are not truly saved.

II.   Trust fund Accounting to Aid Fiscal Policy Planning

This section demonstrates that the trust fund balance is an accounting entry that gives fiscal policy planners information enabling them to easily break down fiscal policy planning into a Social Security part and an independent non-Social Security part. Only if fiscal policy planners rationally utilize that information is the trust fund balance an accurate measure of wealth put aside for the purpose of paying Social Security benefits. In that case, the trust fund is real in the sense that it measures the amount of real wealth put aside to pay future Social Security benefits.

We begin by deriving the government's overall budget constraint, and then break down that constraint into a Social Security part and a non-Social Security part.

A.   The Overall Government Budget Constraint

A fiscal policy is feasible if publicly held debt never gets so large that it is impossible to repay. Publicly held debt in some year t is impossible to repay if choosing maximal primary surpluses in every subsequent year would be insufficient to stabilize debt as a share of GDP. Hence, a feasible fiscal policy is defined by the condition:

(1) $\lim_{k\to\infty} D_k / GDP_k < +\infty,$

where D and GDP denote publicly held debt and GDP, respectively. It is well known that this condition is satisfied if and only if present value of all taxes is at least as large as the present value of all government purchases, where discount rates reflect the actual time profile for the government borrowing rate.[3] Letting T, G, and R denote taxes, government purchases, and the government borrowing rate, respectively, and denoting the first year for which there are any taxes or purchases as year 0, the budget constraint is:

(2) $\lim_{k\to\infty} D_k / GDP_k < +\infty \leftrightarrow \sum_{j=0}^{\infty} T_j \, C_{j\to v} \geq \sum_{j=0}^{\infty} G_j \, C_{j\to v}$

where the valuation year v can be any year and $C_{q\to v}$ is a factor converting year q dollars to year v dollars:

(3) $C_{q\to v} = \Pi_{i=v}^{q-1}(1+R_i)^{-1}$ if $q > v$,

$\qquad = \Pi_{i=q}^{v-1}(1+R_i)$ if $q < v$,

$\qquad = 1$ if $v = q$.

If the possibility that the limiting value of the debt to GDP ratio is infinitely negative is also ruled out, then the present value of taxes must precisely equal the present value of purchases:

(4) $-\infty < \lim_{k\to\infty} D_k / GDP_k < +\infty \leftrightarrow \sum_{j=0}^{\infty} T_j \, C_{j\to v} = \sum_{j=0}^{\infty} G_j \, C_{j\to v}$

At any date t, the budget constraint can also be expressed in terms of debt held by the public at that date and future taxes and purchases:

(5) $-\infty < \lim_{k\to\infty} D_k / GDP_k < +\infty \leftrightarrow \sum_{j=t}^{\infty} T_j \, C_{j\to t} = D_{t-1} + \sum_{j=t}^{\infty} G_j \, C_{j\to t}$

where the valuation year is t and D_{t-1} is debt held by the public at the end of year t-1:

(6) $D_{t-1} = \sum_{j=0}^{t-1} G_j \, C_{j\to t} - \sum_{j=0}^{t-1} T_j \, C_{j\to t}$

---

[3] A derivation is in Mariger (1999).

4

B. Dividing the Budget Into Social Security and Non-Social Security Parts for Planning Purposes

If the budget is divided into two parts, one for Social Security and one for the remainder of government, a sufficient condition for satisfying (5) is that a version of (5) holds for both parts of the budget. Defining T^S as Social Security net taxes that begin in 1937 (benefits are a negative tax), T^O as non-Social Security taxes, and G^O as non-Social Security government purchases, and assuming Social Security purchases are essentially zero, sufficient conditions for a feasible overall fiscal policy (i.e., for (5) to hold) are:

$$(7a) \quad -\infty < \lim_{k \to \infty} D_k^S / GDP_k < +\infty \; \leftrightarrow \; \sum_{j=t}^{\infty} T_j^S \, C_{j \to t} = D_{t-1}^S$$

$$(7b) \quad -\infty < \lim_{k \to \infty} D_k^O / GDP_k < +\infty \; \leftrightarrow \; \sum_{j=t}^{\infty} T_j^O \, C_{j \to t} = D_{t-1}^O + \sum_{j=t}^{\infty} G_j^O \, C_{j \to t}$$

where D_{t-1}^S and D_{t-1}^O are publicly held debt at the end of year t-1 attributable to past Social Security and non- Social Security cash flows, respectively:

$$(8a) \quad D_{t-1}^S = -\sum_{j=0}^{t-1} T_j^S \, C_{j \to t}$$

$$(8b) \quad D_{t-1}^O = \sum_{j=0}^{t-1} (G_j^O - T_j^O) \, C_{j \to t}$$

Adding equations (7a) and (7b) yields (5), so the fiscal balance condition for overall fiscal policy holds if both (7a) and (7b) hold. And because D_{t-1}^S is minus the trust fund balance $(-TFB_{t-1})$, D_{t-1}^O is total publicly held debt plus the trust fund balance:

$$(9a) \quad D_{t-1}^S = -TFB_{t-1}$$

$$(9b) \quad D_{t-1}^O = D_{t-1}^O + D_{t-1}^S - D_{t-1}^S \equiv D_{t-1}^O + D_{t-1}^S + TFB_{t-1} \equiv D_{t-1} + TFB_{t-1}$$

Equations (7a) and (7b) along with (9a) and (9b) are the rationale for Social Security trust fund accounting. If the non-Social Security budget ultimately balances on its own account (i.e., (7b) holds), a necessary and sufficient condition for overall fiscal policy to be feasible is that Social Security cash flows satisfy (7a). Substituting $-TFB_{t-1}$ for D_{t-1}^S in (7a), that budget constraint is:

$$(10) \quad -\infty < \lim_{k \to \infty} TFB_k / GDP_k < \infty \; \leftrightarrow \; AB_\infty \equiv \sum_{j=t}^{\infty} T_j^S \, C_{j \to t} + TFB_{t-1} = 0$$

where AB_∞ is the infinite horizon actuarial balance that is reported each year in the Social Security Trustee Report. Current budget rules are more stringent than (10). Those rules

5

require that the trust fund balance never fall below one year's projected benefit payments, whereas (10) allows for negative trust fund balance provided future Social Security surpluses are sufficient to keep the implied borrowing from the public finite as a share of GDP. While political economy considerations can explain the current prohibition against borrowing against future Social Security tax revenues to pay benefits, that prohibition goes beyond the requirement that Social Security be self-financing. In any case, current budget rules ensure that (10) is satisfied, so it remains true that a sufficient condition for a feasible overall fiscal policy is that Social Security budget rules are satisfied and that non-Social Security policy satisfies (7b).

For the rational planner of non-Social Security policy, (9b) shows that the pertinent debt concept is publicly held debt plus the trust fund balance, which is reported in the federal budget as "gross federal debt." If non-Social Security policy is to be planned independently of Social Security policy, no distinction should be made between how much the non-Social Security budget owes the public and how much it owes the trust fund. If that is in fact the case, the trust fund balance measures the amount by which Social Security cash flows reduce publicly held debt at each point in time, and trust fund accumulations therefore increase the government's capacity to issue public debt in the future to finance benefit payments.

III. Non-Social Security Fiscal Policy Planning

It has been demonstrated that the trust fund balance is merely an accounting entry conveying useful information. It is not a claim on third parties, so somehow losing the information would have no implications for the government's ability to finance its operations going forward. But that fact has no bearing on the question of whether the trust fund represents real wealth. If fiscal policy planners rationally take account of the trust fund accounting information when planning non-Social Security fiscal policy, then the trust fund balance accurately measures wealth accumulated for the purposes of paying future Social Security benefits.

To make these points concrete, this section offers simple models of optimal and suboptimal non-Social Security fiscal policy planning

A. Optimal Forward-Looking Planning of the Non-Social Security Budget

The rational planner of non-Social Security fiscal policy chooses a path for non-Social Security expenditures and taxes that satisfy the budget constraint (7b). This section considers an illustrative optimal non-Social Security fiscal plan that aims to hold the non-Social Security primary surplus share of GDP constant. Absent wars and other temporary special circumstances, such a policy has a reasonable claim of fairly distributing fiscal burdens across generations.

For purposes of calculating this plan, it is useful to bring all terms of (7b) to the left-hand-side and divide by GDP_{t-1}. The budget constraint then becomes:

(11) $\quad d_{t-1}^{O} + \sum_{i=t}^{\infty} s_i^{O}[(1+r)/(1+\eta)]^{t-i} = 0$,

where the real government borrowing rate and the growth rate of real GDP are each assumed to be constant at r and η, respectively; $d_i^{O} = (D_i + TFB_i)/GDP_i$ is the non-Social Security publicly held debt share of GDP; and $s_i^{O} = (T_i^{O} - G_i^{O})/GDP_i$ is the non-Social Security primary surplus share of GDP. Letting $\beta = (1+r)/(1+\eta)$, the constant non-Social Security primary surplus share of GDP satisfying (11) is:

(12) $\quad \tilde{s}_i^{O} = (\beta - 1) d_{t-1}^{O}, i = t, t+1.....$

Noting that $d_i^{O} = \beta d_{i-1}^{O} - s_i^{O}$; $i = t, t+1.....$, it can be verified that the non-Social Security primary surplus rule (10) implies that the non-Social Security debt-to-GDP ratio forever stays constant at d_{t-1}^{O}. This is true only under the assumption that r and η (and hence β) are unchanging over time; otherwise, holding the non-Social Security primary surplus share of GDP constant over time implies a fluctuating non-Social Security debt share of GDP.

Same Plan Formulated Without the Aid of Trust Fund Accounting

Policymakers need not understand trust fund accounting to derive spending rule (11) provided they project Social Security cash flows that are consistent with a self-financing Social Security system. In this case, planners pay attention to the unified budget constraint (5). By analogy with (11), that constraint can be written:

(13) $\quad d_{t-1} + \sum_{i=t}^{\infty} (s_i^{O} + s_i^{S})\beta^{t-i} = 0$

where s_i^{S} is the year-i Social Security primary surplus share of GDP. If the Social Security system is self-financing (i.e., (7b) holds), then:

(14) $\quad \sum_{i=t}^{\infty} s_i^{S}\beta^{t-i} = -TFB_{t-1}/GDP_{t-1}$.

If policymakers make projections for Social Security primary surpluses consistent with (14), then (13) reduces to (11), the budget constraint observed by the planner who understands trust fund accounting.

It is important to understand that this planning method requires projecting Social Security cash flows that are consistent with a self-financing system. If the projected Social Security cash flows were projections of current law scheduled taxes and benefits, then the implied budget constraint for the non-Social Security budget would be too stringent.

B.   A Plausible Suboptimal Non-Social Security Budget Planning Strategy

The rational forward-looking non-Social Security fiscal plan (11) is independent of Social Security fiscal policy, which implies that all Social Security surpluses pay down publicly held debt relative to what would be the case if there had never been a Social Security system.

If Social Security surpluses are not truly saved, then non-Social Security spending and taxes are undoubtedly set with reference to their implications for unified budget totals. A very simple fiscal planning strategy with this property sets non-Social Security primary surpluses so as to target a unified primary surplus equal to some fixed share of GDP in all years. If such a plan starts in year t, then (13) implies it is viable if the unified primary surplus share of GDP is set equal to $d_{t-1}(\beta-1)$ in all years:

(15) $\tilde{s}_j^O + s_j^S = d_{t-1}(\beta-1) \rightarrow \tilde{s}_j^O = d_{t-1}(\beta-1) - s_j^S, \quad j = t, t+1, \ldots.$

This plan implies that publicly held debt forever stays constant as a share of GDP $(d_j = \beta d_{j-1} - (\tilde{s}_j^O + s_j^S) = \beta d_{j-1} - (\beta-1)d_{j-1} = d_{j-1})$. The plan can therefore be expressed:

(16) $\tilde{s}_j^O = d_{j-1}(\beta-1) - s_j^S,$

  $d_j = \beta d_{j-1} - (\tilde{s}_j^O + s_j^S), \quad j = t, t+1, \ldots.$

The fiscal planning strategy (16) is equivalent to the rational forward-looking planning strategy (12) if the Social Security primary surplus share of GDP was to stay constant at its year t level in all future years. In that case, both the Social Security and non-Social Security primary surplus shares of GDP stay forever constant. But the fact is that s^S ultimately declines over time under any reasonable Social Security reform that prefunds exclusively in the trust fund, so the spending rule (16) results in a constant public debt share of GDP and an increasing non-Social Security primary surplus share of GDP. The failure to rationally take account of future Social Security finances results in a suboptimal non-Social Security policy with primary surpluses that grow over time. Growing non-Social Security primary surpluses imply a fiscal policy is more beneficial to current generations and less beneficial to future generations than is the corresponding rational forward-looking plan given by (12).

To generalize (16), it is useful to interpret it as a rational planning strategy under the assumption the Social Security primary surplus will be forever constant at its current level. This interpretation captures the essence of the problem; political constraints prevent invoking austerity measures in the present to prepare for declining Social Security surpluses in the future. It is as if planners pretend that the future budget pressures will not occur. But allowing no foresight beyond the current year is extreme. The federal budget makes projections for five years and sometimes ten years ahead and Congress often invokes procedural rules targeting multi-year budget totals. Hence, we generalize the model so that the non-Social Security surplus share of GDP in year j is set to the level that would be permanently sustainable (i.e., satisfies (13)) if Social Security primary surpluses were to equal actual levels through to year j+N-1 and the actual year j+N-1 level in all subsequent years, where N is a non-negative integer than can be varied. In this case, the model is:

$$(17) \quad \tilde{s}_j^O = (\beta - 1)[d_{j-1} - \sum_{i=j}^{j+N-1} s_i^S \beta^{j-1-i}] - s_{j+N-1}^S \beta^{-N}$$

$$d_j = \beta \, d_{j-1} - \tilde{s}_j^O - s_j^S \qquad\qquad j = t, t+1, \dots$$

This model is such that the non-Social Security primary surplus rises or falls in year j depending on whether projections on which planning is based worsen ($s_{j+N-1}^S < s_{j+N-2}^S$) or improve ($s_{j+N-2}^S > s_{j+N-2}^S$). In a prefunded system, Social Security primary surpluses ultimately fall and adjustments to the non-Social Security primary surplus are on balance positive. As a result, non-Social Security primary surpluses are too low initially and gradually rise over time in response to worsening projections.

Finally, the model is modified to allow for the possibility that politics precludes full upward adjustments to the non-Social Security primary surplus in response to worsening projections. Specifically, the plan is modified to include two regimes given by (17) when (17) calls for an unchanging or declining non-Social Security primary surplus share of GDP,

$$(18a) \quad \hat{s}_t^O = \tilde{s}_t^O \;\; if \;\; \tilde{s}_t^O \le s_{t-1}^O,$$

and which otherwise reverts to a damped version of (17):

$$(18b) \quad \hat{s}_t^O = s_{t-1}^O + \lambda(\tilde{s}_t^O - s_{t-1}^O) \;\; if \;\; \tilde{s}_t^O > s_{t-1}^O,$$

where $\hat{s}_t^O$ is the modified plan, $\tilde{s}_t^O$ refers to the one-regime plan (17), and $\lambda \in [0,1]$ is a parameter reflecting resistance to rises in the non-Social Security primary surplus share of GDP. The debt to GDP ratio evolves according to:

$$(19) \quad d_t = \beta \, d_{t-1} - \hat{s}_t^O - s_t^S$$

The model simulated in Section IV is (17), (18a), (18b), and (19) generalized to allow for time varying β's as documented in Appendix A. The model simulates the time path for the non-Social Security primary surplus share of GDP given an initial value for the debt to GDP ratio and time paths for β and the Social Security primary surplus share of GDP.

IV. Simulated Implications of Not Saving Trust Fund Accumulations

To illustrate the potential importance of taking account of suboptimal fiscal planning when designing a Social Security reform, this section utilizes the Section III fiscal planning model to simulate the response of non-Social Security fiscal policy to two alternative Social Security reforms that differ only with regard to the breakdown of prefunding in the trust fund and prefunding in PRAs. The reforms simulated are the Nonpartisan Reform Plan (NRP) proposed in Liebman, McGuineas, and Samwick (2005), and a version of that plan that prefunds exclusively in the trust fund. The simulations quantify the benefits to future generations of prefunding in PRAs rather than in the trust fund under various assumptions about non-Social Security fiscal policy planning.

NRP calls for substantial cuts to defined benefits that are partly made up by benefits payable from personal retirement account (PRA) balances. PRA contributions are 3 percent of current-law covered earnings, where half of PRA contributions are diversions of payroll tax revenues and half are mandatory out-of-pocket participant contributions. The second plan simulated is the same as NRP except that PRA contributions accumulate in the trust fund and PRA benefits are paid from the trust fund. To isolate the effect PRAs might have on fiscal planning, PRAs are assumed to earn the same rate of return as do trust fund assets.

The Social Security actuary has scored NRP through to 2080 (Social Security Administration, (2005)). After 2080, it is assumed that net contributions to the trust fund and to PRAs are forever constant as a share of GDP and are such that PRA balances and trust fund balances are also constant as shares of GDP. These assumptions of course imply that Social Security is forever self-financing. Estimation details are given in Appendix B.

Figure 1 shows the assumed time path of Social Security primary surpluses under NRP and NRP excluding PRAs (NRP-EX). As total contributions are the same under both plans, the difference between the primary surplus under NRP-EX and NRP is net PRA contributions (gross PRA contributions less benefits payable from PRAs). By construction, both time paths for the Social Security primary surplus are just feasible in the sense that Social Security's infinite horizon actuarial balance is zero.

Total benefits would also be the same under both plans if NRP's PRAs were invested exclusively in federal debt and PRAs do not add to administrative costs. Under those assumptions, the only difference between the plans is that PRA balances under NRP augment trust fund accumulations under NRP-EX, and benefits paid from PRAs under NRP are paid from the trust fund under NRP-EX.

Figure 1 assumes that post-2080 primary surpluses are flat at the levels that put Social Security into an immediate steady state. The NRP primary surplus share of GDP is assumed to drop 0.26 percentage points in 2081 and to then stay constant so as to put the trust fund balance in a steady state equal to 10.6 percent of GDP. As is documented by Table 1, there is no such discontinuity in the assumed primary surplus share of GDP under NRP-EX because of an offsetting discontinuity in NRP's 2081 PRA contributions that occurs by chance. NRP-EX cash flows are equal to NRP's primary surplus plus net contributions to NRP's PRAs, and those net contributions rise by 0.23 percent of GDP in

2081 so as to put the PRA balance share of GDP in a steady state equal to 44.1 percent of GDP.

Figure 2 shows the base-case simulations of the non-Social Security primary surplus time path under both policies starting from 1969 initial conditions for debt and the non-Social Security primary surplus. The simulations assume that the resistance to rising non-Social Security surpluses accords with $\lambda = 0.5$, that the look-ahead period for Social Security surpluses is $N = 5$ years, and that the reform plans are not anticipated until 2007, one year before they affect Social Security cash flows. (See Table 2 for details concerning assumed policymaker expectations). Also, it is assumed that the government borrowing rate (also the assumed trust fund rate of return) and the GDP growth rate accord with actual values through 2004, 2005 Trustee Report projections for 2005 to 2080, and the 2080 Trustee Report values for all years thereafter, and that these values are perfectly anticipated. The government borrowing rate and trust fund return in years prior to 2005 is set equal to the U.S. Treasury one-year constant maturity index for the first week of each fiscal year. Details of how the model generalizes to the case of varying interest rates and GDP growth rates are given in Appendix A.

The simulations are premised on the assumption that the non-Social Security primary surplus share of GDP would be constant if not for the influence of Social Security surpluses. Because this assumption is not generally correct, the simulations should not be expected to track history. What is important is how Social Security policy affects the simulated paths as measured by the difference between the simulations of the optimal path and the suboptimal paths associated with NRP and NRP-EX. It is reasonable to suppose that this difference would be little affected by how policymaker objectives are modeled.

The optimal policy shown in Figure 2 applies to both NRP and NRP-EX. It calls for a constant non-Social Security primary surplus equal to 0.26 percent of GDP. This surplus path is just sufficient to service outstanding debt in 1969 that was attributable to non-Social Security policy, which was 33.8 percent of GDP. (Publicly held debt was 30.2 percent of GDP and the trust fund balance was 3.6 percent of GDP.)

The two suboptimal policies begin diverging in 2007 when Social Security reform is first anticipated. Relative to the optimal path, simulated non-Social Security surpluses are too large between 1969 and 1980 and are too small between 1981 and 2012 under NRP and between 1981 and 2030 under NRP-EX. The brief period of simulated austerity in the non-Social Security budget between 1969 and 1980 is due to negative Social Security primary surpluses between 1973 and 1985 (Figure 1).

Near-term non-Social Security surpluses are much larger under NRP than under NRP-EX. NRP's PRAs reduce the Social Security primary surplus share of GDP by an average of 0.75 percentage points between 2008 and 2047, and the effect on non-Social Security fiscal policy is to increase the non-Social Security primary surplus share of GDP by an average of 0.72 percentage points between 2007 and 2044. As shown in Figure 3,

NRP's PRAs are simulated to reduce debt attributable to non-Social Security policy by about 39 percent of GDP in steady state.

A useful indicator of the intergenerational fairness of non-Social Security policy is the steady-state non-Social Security primary surplus share of GDP. This surplus is 0.43 percent of GDP under NRP and 1.00 percent of GDP under NRP-EX (Figure 2). These surpluses are just sufficient to service steady-state non-Social Security debt, debt that is 30 percent of GDP under NRP and 69 percent of GDP under NRP-EX. By reducing non-Social Security debt accumulation, NRP's PRAs make possible some combination of lower taxes and higher spending that amounts to 0.57 percent of GDP in steady state.

The implications for the steady-state of other assumptions for the inertia parameter λ and the look-ahead period N are reported in Table 3. Higher values of λ result in lower steady-state non-Social Security primary surplus (and non-Social Security debt) under each policy, but the difference between the two policies is only modestly affected by λ. The look-ahead period is more important; relative to the base case, the effect of NRP's PRAs on the simulated steady-state non-Social Security primary surplus is cut by about 19 percent if $N = 10$, and is increased by 14 percent if $N = 1$.

When making judgments as to the most appropriate parameter values, it is important to understand that N and λ are meant to reflect political constraints, not information available to policymakers. Policymakers have all the information they need to optimally plan non-Social Security policy. The optimal non-Social Security policy can be implemented simply by ignoring Social Security surpluses and treating the trust fund balance as a liability to the non-Social Security budget no different than debt held by the public.

A. "Transition Debt" Associated with PRAs

Figure 4 shows that total publicly held debt is a very misleading indicator of the fairness of fiscal policy when PRAs are in the mix. Despite the fact that NRP leads to essentially the same Social Security cash flows for participants and a substantially smaller steady-state non-Social Security primary surplus than NRP-EX, the steady-state publicly held debt to GDP ratio is five percentage points higher under NRP than under NRP-EX. This apparent contradiction is explained by differences in implicit liabilities to pay Social Security defined benefits: This difference—44 percent of GDP in steady state—is the difference between the NRP and NRP-EX optimal time profiles of publicly held debt shown in Figure 4.

Increased publicly held debt is the mechanism by which NRP's PRAs benefit future generations. It is by converting implicit liabilities to pay defined benefits into explicit publicly held debt that policymakers are induced to choose more responsible non-Social Security fiscal policies. And because non-Social Security fiscal policy is more responsible under NRP than NRP-EX, the difference between the suboptimal time profiles of publicly held debt under NRP and NRP-EX is much smaller than the difference between the corresponding optimal profiles.

Ironically, many view the "transition" debt caused by PRAs as a negative. This point of view reflects a simplistic view that the additional publicly held debt necessarily absorbs saving that would otherwise finance real capital investment. This thinking ignores the fact that PRAs directly increase privately managed wealth by precisely the same amount as they increase publicly held debt, so the direct effect of PRAs on capital formation is nil (Mariger, (1999)). And beyond this direct effect on capital formation is an indirect effect–PRAs indirectly increase national saving by encouraging a more prudent non-Social Security fiscal policy. The implication, of course, is that PRAs should cause national saving to rise and interest rates to fall despite the increase in publicly held debt.

The presumption that "transition" debt is undesirable is due to a fundamental misunderstanding of how fiscal policy affects the economy. As Laurence Kotlikoff as argued for many years and in many different contexts, what matters is how fiscal policy transfers wealth across generations, and officially measured deficits and publicly held debt are very imperfect measures of those transfers (e.g., Kotlikoff, Auerbach, and Gokhale (1991)). NRP is more generous to future generations than NRP-EX, yet it results in more steady-state publicly held debt.

As is argued in Section IV, the flawed logic that underlies the notion that transition debt worsens government finances also contributes to policymakers' focus on the unified budget rather than the non-Social Security budget when making fiscal choices.

B.   **Intergenerational Fairness and National Saving**

It is noteworthy that the optimal (and suboptimal) fiscal plans shown in Figures 2-4 are derived without any explicit regard for national saving. Those plans assume that policymakers care only about how fiscal burdens are shared across generations. All policymakers need to know to pursue intergenerational fairness is the time paths for the government borrowing rate and GDP.

How fiscal policy allocates fiscal burdens does nevertheless have important implications for national saving. When deciding how much fiscal burden to impose on current generations relative to future generations, the terms on which those burdens can be traded against each other depend on interest rates. For example, if the real government borrowing rate is always 3 percent, an additional $1 surplus in 2009 makes possible a $4.38 ($1.03^{50}) smaller real surplus in 2059. If policymakers choose to make that trade, increased national saving is the vehicle that makes the trade possible. But policymakers need not concern themselves with those details any more than an individual must concern themselves with national saving when they decide how much to save. They need only concern themselves with whether they have accurately projected rates of return and whether the trade is a good one.

With regard to Figure 3, NRP boosts national saving relative to NRP-EX, and that is reflected in the lower steady-state non-Social Security primary surplus. Specifically, the reduced steady-state primary surplus is precisely the annual dividend made possible by the increased national saving.

The time path of national saving does have some direct importance for policy choices because it helps determine the time paths of interest rates and GDP. However, the feedback of national saving on interest rates and GDP actually attenuates the amount of national saving a fiscal policy targeting intergenerational fairness generates. In general, shifting fiscal burdens from future generations to current generations causes national savings to rise, interest rates to fall, and future GDP to rise. Both feedback effects cause policymakers to want to put less fiscal burden on current generations, as the feedback effects of increasing the fiscal burden on current generations make future generations wealthier and worsen the terms on which current fiscal burdens substitute for future fiscal burdens (Cutler, Poterba, Sheiner, and Summers, (1990)). By causing policymakers to place less fiscal burden on current generations and more on later generations, feedback effects attenuate the amount of national saving the plan generates.

A recent analysis in Diamond and Orszag (2004) illustrates the fallacy of thinking in terms of national saving rather than intergenerational fairness when evaluating fiscal policy. When considering whether Social Security surpluses are truly saved, those authors argue that what matters is how Social Security surpluses affect both government saving and private saving. They argue that to the extent that Social Security surpluses are offset by smaller non-Social Security surpluses, the negative implications are muted to the extent that private saving increases as a result. They then offer a scenario where such increases in private saving come about via changes in the distribution of taxes within generations. But even if the suggested scenario were true, changes in savings that come about because of changes in the distribution of taxes *within* generations can do little to ameliorate the implications of fiscal policy for the distribution of net taxes *between* generations that are shown in Figure 3.[4]

V.   Thirty Years of Budget Politics

Given that so much rides on the question of whether or not trust fund accumulations pay down federal debt, it is important to carefully consider the evidence. That evidence is of two general types: formal analysis of historical budget data, and informal observations of budget politics. Mariger (2008) considers the budget data and concludes that it weakly supports the hypothesis that trust fund accumulations are largely offset by increased non-Social Security deficits. That evidence is weak because there is little independent year-to-year variation in Social Security surpluses, which makes it difficult to get precise

---

[4] Imposing a larger fiscal burden on current generations so that a lower fiscal burden is imposed on future generations benefits future generations because they pay lower net taxes and less importantly because increased national saving increases their wages. Inducing current generations to save more on their own account can benefit future generations only via the less important second channel. Moreover, additional national saving comes about from reduced near-term national consumption, and that reduction in national consumption is shorter lived when it is due to individuals consuming less early in life so they can consume more later in life than if it is due to current generations consuming less so that distant future generations can consume more.

statistical measures of how those surpluses influence other variables. The most definitive evidence therefore stems from recent budget deliberations.

The remainder of this section is organized into two subsections. The first subsection offers some conjectures on what policymakers and voters must know in order to save Social Security surpluses. That discussion suggests that the level of sophistication demonstrated by policymakers is a relevant part of recent budget history. The second subsection discusses specific post-1980 fiscal policy developments.

A. What Policymakers and Voters Must Know in Order to Save Social Security Surpluses

In order to truly save Social Security surpluses, it is reasonable to infer that policymakers and voters must understand how trust fund accounting information can be used to plan Social Security and non-Social Security policy entirely independently of each other (Section III). With that understanding, non-Social Security policy would be planned with reference to its implications for the path of gross federal debt—debt held by the public and by the trust fund—and annual changes in that debt concept—the non-Social Security deficit. While it is possible to rationally plan non-Social Security policy in the context of the unified budget (Section III), that approach adds the unnecessary complication of projecting primary Social Security surpluses associated with a *solvent* system. Someone understanding the second planning method would also understand the first, and hence would elect the relatively easy first option.

There is little evidence that policymakers or budget experts view trust fund accounting as information useful for planning non-Social Security fiscal policy. To the contrary, several reputable sources describe trust fund accounting in a way that suggests it has no useful purpose other than to automatically authorize Social Security benefit payments. Descriptions of the trust funds offered in recent Congressional testimony given by the Congressional Budget Office and the General Accountability Office are very similar to the description that has been in the Federal budget since at least 1997:

> The holdings of the trust funds are not assets of the Government as a whole that can be drawn down in the future to fund benefits. Instead, they are claims on the Treasury. When trust fund holdings are redeemed to pay benefits, Treasury will have to finance the expenditure in the same way as any other Federal expenditure: out of current receipts, by borrowing from the public, or by reducing benefits or other expenditures. The existence of large trust fund balances, therefore, does not, **by itself** [emphasis added], increase the Government's ability to pay benefits. [5]

---

[5] Federal Budget FY2008, Analytical Perspectives, p. 345; Government Accountability Office (2005), p. 2; Congressional Budget Office testimony cited in footnote 1. The General Accountability Office testimony qualifies its description with the heading: "trust fund solvency **alone** is not sufficient" but does not explain the circumstances under which trust fund solvency implies true solvency. The Congressional Budget Office testimony offers no qualifiers. As the FY1997 budget includes essentially the same statement as the FY2008 budget, it is inferred that all intervening budgets did as well.

The key qualifier "by itself" is not explained. The debate over the meaning of trust fund accounting would be greatly elevated if it were explained that "by itself" translates to "holding publicly held debt constant," that trust fund accumulations do in fact increase the government's capacity to pay benefits if they pay down publicly held debt, and that if Social Security surpluses pay down publicly held debt dollar for dollar, then the trust fund balance at each date is a precise measure of the amount by which Social Security has reduced publicly held debt.

Also telling is the fact that OMB and CBO do not provide information necessary to plan non-Social Security policy independently of Social Security policy, at least not on a regular basis. Their long-range budget analyses exclusively take a unified perspective. In those analyses, Social Security revenues and outlays are lumped with other revenues and outlays for purposes of measuring fiscal imbalances, and policymakers are offered no metric of how much non-Social Security fiscal policy must change to make it alone sustainable. (For example, see Congressional Budget Office (2005) and Office of Management and Budget (2002).)

In one special case—when there are baseline unified surpluses—policymakers and voters act as though they comprehend what it means to save Social Security surpluses in the context of a unified budget. In that case, it is relatively easy to infer that the unified surplus up to the amount of the Social Security surplus is saved for Social Security. But while this perceived understanding potentially enables Social Security surpluses to be saved, the understanding is flawed, as it is possible to save the entire Social Security surplus while running a unified surplus substantially smaller than the Social Security surplus. This latter possibility can be comprehended only when thinking in terms a non-Social Security budget that is entirely separate from the Social Security budget.

B.   Specific Budget Developments

Gramm-Rudman-Hollings

The Balanced Budget and Emergency Deficit Control Act of 1985 (Gramm-Rudman-Hollings) was a desperate attempt to get deficits down from unprecedented peacetime levels. The Act set unified deficit targets for FY1987 to FY1991 that steadily declined and reached $0 in FY1991. The targets were revised up and extended to FY1993 in a 1987 amendment, and again the terminal target was $0. The fact that the targets were in terms of unified rather than non-Social Security deficits is telling. Blinder (1990) and others have argued that the targets could easily have been non-Social Security deficit targets that were translated to unified targets, but if that were so, why didn't the targets extend further into the future and terminate at a unified surplus equal to the projected Social Security surplus? And expressing non-Social Security deficit targets in terms of unified deficit targets has a cost, as projection errors for Social Security surpluses illogically relax or strengthen the implied non-Social Security deficit targets.

It might be argued that because the Gramm-Rudman-Hollings deficit targets were not met, it would not have made any difference what Congress or voters thought was the best measure of fiscal prudence. This view is taken by Diamond and Orszag (2004). They suggest that the deficit reduction in the late 1980s and early 1990s "was driven mostly by the qualitative view that the deficit was excessive, instead of being calibrated to the exact size of some measure of the deficit" and therefore "it seems plausible to us that increases in the Social Security surplus did not generate significant increases in the non-Social Security deficit." This argument seemingly denies any rationality in the choice of target and actual deficits. If the target and actual deficits were rationally chosen, they'd take account of the fact that each person's most preferred policy equates the perceived marginal benefits and costs of deficit reduction, and the perceived marginal benefits of deficit reduction would surely be larger if perceived fiscal prudence corresponded with the non-Social Security deficit than if it corresponded to the unified deficit.

The Threat to Return Social Security To Pay-As-You-Go Financing

The bipartisan *National Economic Commission* was created by Congress in 1987 to recommend ways to reduce the federal deficit. It included two Senators, two House members, and ten members from the private sector. As the Republican and Democratic members could not find common ground, the 1989 report was split into a Republican Majority Report and a Democratic Minority Report. The concluding section of the Minority Report included this statement:

> Let no one suppose that a Democratic Congress will much longer allow a payroll tax to be used to service a $2 to $3 trillion debt owned in vastly disproportionate amounts by wealthy individuals and institutions. It already requires nearly one-half the revenues of the income tax to pay interest. This surely is the largest transfer of wealth from labor to capital in the history of our political arithmetic. But at least this is a graduated tax. By 1992 the trust fund reserves will have reached 100 percent of annual outlays; a considerable reserve. By 1994 the proportion reaches 150 percent. If, in the next five years, no arrangements are made to save the future incomes of the funds, Congress – you may depend on it – will return to pay-as-you-go financing.

Two years later, Senator Moynihan, a Democratic member of the Commission, introduced a bill in the Senate Finance Committee that would have made good on this threat. The bill would have increased the maximum taxable payroll and adjusted tax rates so as to achieve approximate pay-as-you-go financing of Social Security benefits. The bill had ten sponsors and cosponsors, four of them Republicans. The identical companion bill in the House had 37 sponsors and cosponsors, 14 of them Republicans. Neither bill got out of committee.[6]

The Push for a Balanced Budget Amendment to the U.S. Constitution

The fact that the Gramm-Rudman-Hollings deficit targets were expressed in terms of unified deficits rather than non-Social Security deficits might be excused by the fact that substantial Social Security surpluses were a relatively new phenomenon. But a proposed 1995 Balanced Budget Amendment to the Constitution that was passed the House of

---

[6] S.11 and HR.524 were both introduced to their respective Houses of Congress on January 14, 1991.

Representatives and was narrowly defeated in the Senate also targeted unified budget balance. It is probable the amendment would have passed in the Senate if it had been modified to appease some Democrats who wished to target non-Social Security budget balance rather than unified balance so as to protect Social Security from austerity measures.[7] The same dispute arose in a 1997 Senate debate over a proposed balanced budget amendment. Republicans were again opposed to targeting non-Social Security budget balance. The Republican Chairmen of the Senate and House Budget committees offered objections suggesting a profound misunderstanding what it means to save Social Security surpluses and what would be gained:[8]

> "If it is true that excluding Social Security from the balanced-budget amendment would force us to "save" the short-term surplus, it is equally true that excluding Social Security would allow us to run massive budget deficits... beginning in 2019 ....Ironically, these massive and unprecedented deficits would be specifically sanctioned by an amendment to the Constitution." (Pete V. Domenici, Senate Budget Committee Chairman)

> "There are no trust funds. There's not a stack of bonds, there's IOUs." (John R. Kasich, House Budget Committee Chairman.)

Of course, the point of saving the Social Security surpluses is to make room for publicly held debt issuance (i.e., deficits) when the old-age dependency ratio is higher than it is at the time of the surpluses. And while the trust funds might be just IOUs not representing real saving under the status quo, the point of a balanced budget amendment for the non-Social Security budget is to ensure that Social Security surpluses are in fact saved.

"Save Social Security First" – The Clinton FY2000 Budget

The Clinton FY2000 budget projected baseline unified surpluses in every year of the ten-year budget window extending to FY2009 and non-Social Security surpluses starting in FY2001. In order to "save Social Security first," the budget proposed to transfer 62 percent of the unified surplus in the FY2000-FY2014 period to the trust fund despite the fact that most of the projected unified surplus were Social Security surpluses that would be credited the trust fund once already.[9] Three Administration insiders explain this as a strategy for avoiding the logical alternative means of preserving Social Security surpluses: Start with the baseline non-Social Security surpluses and explicitly allocate them to various policy proposals (Elmendorf, Liebman, and Wilcox (2001)). This latter strategy was rejected because the Administration's policy proposals were too expensive and would have dissipated not only the baseline non-Social Security surpluses but also some of the Social Security surpluses. Either the Administration thought that making proposals that would eat into Social Security surpluses was not consistent with saving Social Security surpluses (not necessarily true), or they thought voters would think so.

---

[7] Wildavsky and Caiden (1997), p. 303.
[8] Congressional Quarterly Weekly Report (1997)
[9] The budget included baseline surplus estimates for only ten years. Over that period, 70 percent of the projected unified surpluses were Social Security surpluses.

As a result of stronger-than-expected receipts in the first half of 1999, the FY2000 Midsession Review boosted the baseline ten-year unified surplus projection 21 percent above the levels projected in the budget. This development enabled a revised budgeting strategy. Social Security surpluses would be preserved in their entirely, and non-Social Security surpluses would be explicitly allocated to various uses. One line item in the allocation of non-Social Security surpluses was a general revenue transfer to the trust fund equal to the estimated net interest savings that would come about if the post-1999 Social Security surpluses paid down federal debt. Unacknowledged in the Midsession Review or in Elmendorf, Liebman, and Wilcox (2001) is the fact that this would also constitute a double-credit to the trust fund, as interest paid to the trust fund represents net interest savings that come about if Social Security surpluses pay down federal debt.

The Administration presumably made a calculated decision to obscure the issues to increase the likelihood that the baseline surpluses would be preserved. But those tactics could have been effective only for as long as there were baseline unified surpluses that could be allocated in part to Social Security. Once projected baseline unified surpluses disappeared, policymakers and voters were again without clear guidelines as to what it means to save Social Security surpluses. If the Administration had instead proposed planning non-Social Security policy based on gross federal debt and its year-to-year changes, its PR campaign might have had a more lasting effect.

Social Security "Lock Boxes"

The Republican response to the Clinton save-social-security-first campaign was Social Security "lock-boxes." The more stringent proposed lock-box mechanisms called for creating a limit on debt held by the public in addition to the current limit that applies to gross public debt (publicly held debt plus trust fund debt). The proposed limit on debt held by the public would have declined in accordance with projected Social Security surpluses (Koitz, Kollmann and Nuschler (2001)). It is revealing that an equivalent and simpler mechanism for achieving the same end was not proposed–set unchanging limits on gross publicly held debt. If it was understood that gross publicly held debt is the pertinent debt concept for planning non-Social Security fiscal policy, this second option would have been the natural choice.

Like with the Clinton Administration approach to saving Social Security surpluses, Lock Boxes aren't a useful tool for saving Social Security surpluses when baseline unified surpluses are negative. In that case, the artificial bright line between saving and not saving Social Security surpluses (when the unified surplus is larger or smaller than the Social Security surplus) disappears and fiscal policy is once again without clear navigational beacons.

The Return to Baseline Unified Deficits

The G.W. Bush Administration initially adopted a policy of maintaining unified surpluses at least as large as Social Security surpluses. But this policy was abandoned when the economy went into recession and national security outlays increased after the September 11, 2001 terrorist attacks. The 2003 tax cuts were justified by Republicans as a means to lift the economy out of recession, but there was no impetus from Republicans to restore the lost revenues after the economy recovered. Likewise, the increase in national security expenditures was largely permanent, yet there was little effort to find permanent offsets.

Also revealing is the fact that the Administration's deficit reduction targets have been stated in terms of the unified deficit rather than the on-budget deficit. Specifically, the goal set in the FY2005 federal budget was to achieve a FY2009 unified deficit half as large as the FY2004 unified deficit.

The Recent Social Security Reform Debate

The debate spawned by the G.W. Bush administration's Social Security reform efforts has exposed fundamental misunderstanding of how Social Security affects long-term fiscal balance and the economy. Specifically, the meaning of the date when Social Security's cash flows first become negative–currently projected to be 2017—has been confused, as has the meaning of so-called "transition debt" associated with introducing PRAs. These confusions cast serious doubt on the possibility that policymakers and voters understand what it means to plan non-Social Security policy independently of Social Security policy.

Policymakers who believe Social Security surpluses are not saved invariably measure the Social Security's fiscal imbalance with reference to Social Security's cash flows rather than the trust fund balance. For example, the August 2000 interim report of the President's Commission to Strengthen Social Security states: "In 2016, the program's benefit obligations will exceed its annual tax revenue. While the government will continue to pay benefits, 2016 is the beginning of a long-term financing problem for the government." The point of this statement is that Social Security reform is more urgent than the trust fund balance projections suggest. Recent General Accountability Office congressional testimony makes the same point (General Accountability Office (2005)).

As it stands, this thinking leads to contradictions. It would imply that reforms that divert payroll tax revenues to PRAs and reduce defined benefits in an actuarially fair manner would worsen long-term fiscal imbalances. It would also imply that increasing payroll tax revenues so as to postpone the negative cash flow date would improve long-term federal finances. But assuming Social Security surpluses are not saved, both inferences are wrong. In the first instance, the government's long-term finances are entirely unaffected except that non-Social Security surpluses would presumably rise. In the second instance, the additional revenues only make it possible for non-Social Security policy to be irresponsible for longer.

The problem with simply citing the negative cash flow date as an indicator of Social Security's financial imbalance is that it gets the timing of fiscal problems wrong and it confuses imbalance in the non-Social Security budget for imbalances in the Social Security budget. If the premise that Social Security surpluses are not saved is accepted, then the negative cash flow date does not signal the beginning of fiscal problems; the fiscal problem is that Social Security surpluses now, in the past, and in the future cause correspondingly lower non-Social Security surpluses. It is an ongoing problem, and it is a non-Social Security budget problem that has only been facilitated by Social Security budget policy.

The simulations of the Social Security reform NRP-EX in Section IV make these points concrete. Recall that this plan relies on trust fund accumulations to make Social Security nominally solvent. Under that plan, the Social Security primary surplus share of GDP stays about flat through to 2017 and then commences a steady decline, turning negative in 2033 and reaching a steady state of –0.8 percent in 2080 (Figure 1). Prior to the steady state, near-term Social Security primary surpluses are always larger than surpluses in the more distant future, and this causes policymakers to choose a smaller non-Social Security primary surplus than they would if they had better foresight. The problem, summarized by publicly held debt attributable to non-Social Security policy as a share of GDP (Figure 3), gets ever worse before peaking in steady-state. Nothing special happens in 2033 when the Social Security primary surplus turns negative.

The fixation with Social Security's negative cash flow date reflects a more general fixation with cash flows and publicly held debt as indicators of the stance of fiscal policy. Currently, it appears that Social Security is greatly holding down federal liabilities. But any reasonable measure of the Social Security benefit accruals would show that current Social Security liabilities far exceed outstanding publicly held debt. If it were understood that Social Security benefit promises are an implicit liability that have approximately the same implications for the economy and long-term fiscal balance as do explicit liabilities taking the form of publicly held debt, it would be understood that the government's fiscal problems are ongoing and that the negative cash flow date has little significance.[10]

The belief that the key fiscal policy indicators are cash flows and publicly held debt is also at the root of misguided concern about "transition debt" associated with PRAs. For example, the PRAs proposed in the G.W. Bush FY2007 budget would have subtracted substantially from the government's near- and mid-term cash flows but would nevertheless have left the government's long-term fiscal position only slightly compromised. For every dollar contributed to the PRA, publicly held debt would rise by a dollar, but the present value of the government's obligations to pay defined benefits would be reduced by about $0.94.[11]   And the $0.06 net worsening of the government's

---

[10] Because publicly held debt is tradable and promises to pay defined benefits are non-tradable, there may be some second-order differences in the economic implications of implicit and explicit government liabilities.

[11] The Administration's proposed PRAs would have been combined with cuts in traditional benefits equal to the annuity value of a notional PRA balance computed as if PRAs earned an annual return 0.3 percentage points less than the real government borrowing rate. Assuming a 3 percent real government borrowing rate and real PRA contributions growing at a 1.1 percent annual rate between age 25 and 65, an individual's

long-term budget balance would presumably be made up with other Social Security reforms. Yet many if not most policymakers expected that this transition debt would have the same effects on the economy and government finances as would debt issued for the purposes of financing additional federal purchases. Even presumably disinterested professional economists at the International Monetary Fund offered this assessment:

> "The Administration's proposal for personal retirement accounts (PRAs) would not help place the system on a sustainable basis and would significantly raise federal deficits and debt in coming decades." (International Monetary Fund (2005))

Despite prodding from U.S. Treasury staff, the IMF document made no attempt to explain that the proposed PRAs would have reduced the government's implicit liabilities by almost as much as it increases its explicit liabilities.

The fact that many PRA supporters are concerned about transition debt is especially curious. The major advantage of PRAs is that they increase unified deficits so that they better approximate the annual net increase in true government liabilities while not changing those liabilities. It is only by increasing unified deficits so as to make policymakers better aware of the true state of fiscal policy that PRAs would facilitate a more responsible non-Social Security budget policy.

VI. Implications for Social Security Reform

If trust fund accumulations are not truly saved, then the possibilities for making Social Security fair to future generations are greatly limited. Large dividends would be paid, therefore, if an alternative effective prefunding mechanism could be found. Full-fledged PRAs are only one such option. But other possibilities exist. For example, simple no-frills PRAs invested exclusively in federal debt and administered by a semi-autonomous government entity very possibly would succeed at making it obvious to policymakers and voters that the PRA balances are not available to fund non-Social Security programs.

If political constraints dictate that attempted prefunding take place in the trust fund, and if such prefunding is offset with smaller non-Social Security surpluses, then it would be rational to skew Social Security reform in the direction of limiting trust fund accumulations in a manner that benefits future generations. Relative to a first-best reform with effective prefunding, it is argued below that a second-best policy with ineffective prefunding calls for lower benefits levels. The argument has two parts: First, two high level policy choices that determine the level of trust fund accumulations are identified, and then the effects on the welfare of future generations of modifying those choices are analyzed.

---

notional PRA balance at retirement would be 94 percent as large as the increase in federal debt attributable to the individual's lifetime PRA contributions.

Two Key High-Level Policy Choices

It is shown in Mariger (1999) that Social Security's payroll taxes can be interpreted as a combination of forced saving and pure taxes necessary to service an implicit government debt that arose because of wealth transfers made to generations that now are either retired or deceased (roughly individuals born prior to 1930). For example, if an individual pays lifetime payroll taxes with a present value of $200,000 and receives lifetime benefits with a present value of $150,000, then the $200,000 of lifetime payroll taxes divide into $150,000 of forced saving and a $50,000 pure tax. Note that the level of forced saving determines the level of benefits.[12]

Two key Social Security policy decisions are: (1) How should the pure taxes necessary to service Social Security's implicit debt burden be distributed across the generations that will be subject to reform, and (2) how large should be benefits (forced saving). Together, these two choices determine the amount and timing of trust fund accumulations. Relative to a first-best reform, the choices can be skewed so as to reduce trust fund accumulations if benefit levels are reduced while holding pure tax burdens constant, or if the share of the Social Security pure tax burden that is imposed on early birth cohorts is reduced while keeping benefit levels constant. However, as is discussed below, only the first method of reducing trust fund accumulations would benefit future generations.

Reducing Benefit Levels While Holding Pure Tax Burdens Constant

An inability to prefund Social Security benefits has an important effect on the decision of how large to make benefits. Compared with a reform that would be best overall if trust fund accumulations were truly saved, lowering each person's taxes paid while working and benefits received in retirement in an actuarially fair manner (that is, reducing forced saving) would greatly reduce trust fund accumulations without affecting Social Security's solvency or changing the distribution of Social Security's pure taxes across birth cohorts or income groups within birth cohorts. This policy change would have little effect on the well-being or retirement incomes of individuals who increase their private saving by the amount of their tax reductions— such people would do less forced saving through Social Security but make it up by saving more on their own. Individuals who do not save their tax reductions, however, might have inadequate income in retirement. That downside must be weighed against the increased fairness of overall fiscal policy toward future generations.

---

[12] What is important for this discussion is pure taxes and forced saving aggregated across members of the various birth cohorts. For birth cohorts, Social Security will levy a positive pure tax on all birth cohorts. It is worth noting, however, that the division of Social Security payroll taxes into pure taxes and forced saving makes sense for a low-income individual receiving a net lifetime transfers from Social Security. Such an individual receives lifetime transfers from other members of his or her birth cohort, and forced saving is equal to payroll taxes plus transfers received.

Changing the Distribution of the Pure Tax Burdens While Holding Benefit Levels Constant

Suppose the level of benefits (that is, forced saving) is held constant. Then trust fund accumulations could be reduced by shifting pure tax burdens only if payroll taxes were reduced for early birth cohorts and increased for later birth cohorts. But while this policy would reduce trust fund accumulations, it clearly would not benefit future generations.[13]

VII. Summary and Conclusion

The essential points made in this paper are:

- Trust fund accounting is merely accounting, but accounting that matters if policymakers and voters understand how it can be used to independently plan Social Security and non-Social Security fiscal policy.

- If non-Social Security policy is planned independently of Social Security policy, then: (i) the trust fund balance at each date is a precise measure of how much Social Security has reduced publicly held debt as of that time, (ii) by reducing publicly held debt issuance when the old-age dependency ratio is relatively low, Social Security surpluses make it possible to issue additional publicly held debt in the future to help pay Social Security benefits when the old-age dependency ratio is relatively high, and (iii) the trust fund, while not itself constituting financial claims on third parties, accurately measures real wealth that has been put aside to pay future Social Security benefits.

- Whether or not Social Security surpluses are saved has extremely important implications for fiscal policy planning. If Social Security surpluses are not saved, then Social Security reform that relies on trust fund accumulations to make Social Security fair across generations is neutralized by a non-Social Security fiscal policy that is less fair across generations. In this case, large dividends would be paid if an effective alternative means of prefunding Social Security could be found.

- Non-Social Security policy can be independent of Social Security policy only if non-Social Security budget decisions are guided solely by their implications for gross federal debt (publicly held debt plus the trust fund balance) and its changes as measured by the non-Social Security deficit. This would imply that planners of non-Social Security policy view non-Social Security liabilities held by the trust fund as every bit as real as debt held by the public.

- If planners of non-Social Security policy view Social Security surpluses as reducing the need to reduce non-Social Security deficits, then Social Security

---

[13] However, it is worth noting that shifting the payroll tax burden from early to later generations would also not harm later generations if trust fund accumulations are not truly saved. To see this, suppose payroll taxes are reduced in the near term and increased in the longer term so that the present value of payroll tax revenues is unchanged, and that the near-term payroll tax increases are exactly offset by higher non- Social Security revenues in every year. Then the amount of publicly held debt that future generations inherit would not be changed, and nor would their benefit payment obligations. It follows that those generations are made no better or worse off by the policy change.

surpluses are not wholly saved. The perception of a reduced need to reduce non-Social Security deficits might be due to an illusion that current Social Security surpluses are more permanent than they are, or an illusion that the unified deficit is a better measure of fiscal policy's effect on the economy than is the non-Social Security deficit.

- A common-sense interpretation of recent budget history suggests that the odds that Social Security surpluses are not saved are very significant.
- If political constraints demand that Social Security prefunding be attempted in the trust fund and such prefunding is undone with smaller non-Social Security surpluses, then it would be rational to compromise other Social Security reform objectives so as to reduce such attempted prefunding. Specifically, relative to a first-best reform with effective prefunding, smaller benefit levels would be appropriate.

Appendix A
The Simulation Model Generalized to the Case of Varying
Interest Rates and GDP Growth Rates

To ease exposition, the Section III models specialize to case where the real government borrowing rate and the growth rate of real GDP are constant. The simulations in Section IV, on the other hand, assume historical values for these variables through to 2004 and projections thereafter and hence are based on a more general model that is derived in this appendix.

The Non-Social Security Budget Constraint

A straight-forward generalization of the non-Social Security budget constraint (11) is:

$$\text{(A1)} \quad d_{t-1}^O + \sum_{i=t}^{\infty} s_i^O \, [\textstyle\prod_{k=t}^{i} \beta_k^{-1}] = 0$$

where $\beta_k = (1+r_k)/(1+\eta_k)$ depends on the year-k real government borrowing rate r_k and real GDP growth rate η_k.

The Optimal Non-Social Security Primary Surplus Path

The constant non-Social Security surplus share of GDP satisfying (A1) is:

$$\text{(A2)} \quad \tilde{s}_i^O = z_t d_{t-1}^O, i = t, t+1.....$$

where the series $z_m^{-1} = \sum_{j=m}^{\infty} \prod_{k=m}^{j} \beta_k^{-1}$, $m = t, t+1,....$ and z_m, $m = t, t+1,....$ can be calculated recursively as follows:

$$\text{(A3)} \quad z_{m-1}^{-1} = \beta_{m-1}^{-1}(1 + \sum_{j=m}^{\infty} \prod_{k=m}^{j} \beta_k^{-1}) = \beta_{m-1}^{-1}(1 + z_m^{-1}) \leftrightarrow z_{m-1} = \beta_{m-1}(1 + z_m^{-1})^{-1}$$

Once in steady-state with β unchanging, z is also unchanging and equal to $\beta - 1$. Working back from the first steady-state year, the entire time profile for z can be computed using (A3).

Suboptimal Non-Social Security Primary Surplus Path When There is No Budget Inertia

The $\lambda = 1$ suboptimal non-Social Security primary surplus path $\tilde{s}_m^O$, $m = t, t+1,....$ is planned in the context of the unified budget constraint. By analogy with (A1), that budget constraint is:

$$\text{(A4)} \quad d_{t-1} + \sum_{i=t}^{\infty} (s_i^O + s_i^S)[\textstyle\prod_{k=t}^{i} \beta_k^{-1}] = 0$$

The simulation model assumes the planner makes accurate projections of the Social Security primary surplus for years t, t+1, …, t+N-1, but assumes surpluses beyond year t+N-1 are equal to the year t-N-1 projection. Hence, the planned non-Social Security primary surplus for year t $\tilde{s}_t^O$ satisfies:

$$\text{(A5)} \quad d_{t-1} + \sum_{i=t}^{t+N-1} s_i^S \left[\prod_{k=t}^{i} \beta_k^{-1}\right] + s_{t+N-1}^S z_{t+N-1}^{-1} + \tilde{s}_t^O z_t^{-1} = 0$$

which implies:

$$\text{(A6)} \quad \tilde{s}_t^O = -z_t \left[d_{t-1} + \sum_{i=t}^{t+N-1} s_i^S \left[\prod_{k=t}^{i} \beta_k^{-1}\right] + s_{t+N-1}^S z_{t+N-1}^{-1} \right]$$

Suboptimal Non-Social Security Primary Surplus Path When $0 < \lambda < 1$

If there is resistance to increases in the non-Social Security primary surplus, then the suboptimal plan takes the form:

$$\text{(A7)} \quad \hat{s}_t^O = \tilde{s}_t^O \text{ if } \hat{s}_t^O \geq \tilde{s}_t^O$$
$$\hat{s}_t^O = s_{t-1}^O + \lambda(\tilde{s}_t^O - s_{t-1}^O) \text{ if } \tilde{s}_t^O < s_{t-1}^O$$

Appendix B
Social Security Primary Surplus Projections Under NRP and NRP-EX

I. NRP Estimates

The Social Security actuary has made 75-year projections of NRP's effects on government cash flows and trust fund balances (Social Security Administration (2005)).

The simulation model assumes that the annual government borrowing rate and the trust fund yield are the same, as must be true if the government's overall budget constraint divides neatly into a Social Security part and a non- Social Security part. For the period 1969-2004, this return is measured as the U.S. Treasury constant one-year constant maturity index for the first week of each fiscal year. As this rate is not precisely the same as the trust fund yield, simulated historical trust fund balances do not equal actual balances. In 2004, the simulated trust fund balance share of GDP is 11.4 percent, which compares with the actual balance equal to 14.4 percent.

After 2004, the government borrowing rate and the trust fund return are set to the 2005 Trustee Report projections for the trust fund return.

In 2080, projections of the trust fund balance and the primary surplus as shares of GDP are 10.56 percent and 0.11 percent, respectively. To put Social Security in an immediate steady-state in 2081, it is assumed the primary surplus share of GDP falls to -0.15 percent in that year and forever stays at that level.

II. NRP-EX Estimates

NRP-EX makes NRP's PRA cash flows part of government cash flows. Hence, government cash flows under NRP-EX are NRP cash flows explained above plus NRP PRA cash flows.

NRP's PRA cash flows are based on the Social Security actuary's projections for PRA contributions and PRA balances through to 2080. Given contributions to PRAs, PRA balances, and the assumed PRA rate of return, it is possible to back out estimates of benefits paid from PRAs. The PRA benefit estimates are then multiplied by a factor of 1.067 to adjust to the assumption that PRAs earn the same return as the trust funds. That estimate is based on the evolution of PRA balances for a hypothetical individual whose real contributions grow at 1.1 percent annually between ages 25 and 65 and who either earns a 2.7 percent real annual return (the Social Security actuary's assumption) or a 3.0 percent real annual return (the assumed real government borrowing rate). The age-65 PRA balance is 6.7 percent higher in the latter case than in the former.

In 2080, projections of PRA balances and net contributions as shares of GDP are 42.47 percent and -0.89 percent, respectively. To put the PRAs in an immediate steady-state in 2081, it is assumed the net contribution share of GDP rises to -0.62 percent in that year and forever stays at that level.

Table 1
Post-2080 Steady-State Assumptions*
(Percent of GDP)

NRP Component	2080 Inferences		2081+ Steady State	
	Primary Surplus*	Prefunding Balance**	Primary Surplus	Prefunding Balance**
NRP Trust Fund	0.11	10.56	-0.15	10.56
NRP PRAs	-0.87	44.11	-0.64	44.11
NRP-EX Trust Fund = NRP + NRP PRAs	-0.76	54.67	-0.80	54.67

*PRA primary surplus equals actuary's estimate of contributions less inferred PRA benefits. PRA benefits are inferred from actuary's estimated PRA balances, contributions, and rate of return equal to the Trust Fund return less 0.3 percentage points, and are then augmented by 7 percent to account for the assumption of a 0.3 percentage point higher annual rate of return.

**PRA balances are inferred from net PRA contributions (see * above) and an assumed rate of return equal to the Trust Fund rate of return.

Table 2
Policymaker Expectation of Social Security Primary Surpluses
Within the Look-Ahead Period

Year Expectation Held	Year in Which Look-Ahead Period Expected Surplus Occurs		
	1970-2004	2005-2007	2008+
1970-2006	Actual values	2005 Trustee Report projections* = assumed actuals	2005 Trustee Report projections*
2007+	na	na	Actuary's scorings of reform plans = assumed actuals

*2005 Trustee Report projections are assumed because the actuary's scorings of NRP is based on the economic and demographic assumptions of that report.

Table 3
Simulated Steady-State Non-Social Security Surplus and Publicly-Held Debt
Attributable to Non-Social Security Policy
(Percent of GDP)

Look Ahead Period N (Years)	NRP, Inertia Parameter λ=			NRP-EX, Inertia Parameter λ=			NRP-EX Less NRP, Inertia Parameter λ=		
	0.1	0.5	1	0.1	0.5	1	0.1	0.5	1
--------Non-Social Security Surplus--------									
1	0.70	0.43	0.39	1.40	1.08	1.03	0.70	0.65	0.64
5	0.66	0.43	0.40	1.27	1.00	0.96	0.61	0.57	0.56
10	0.65	0.44	0.41	1.17	0.90	0.87	0.51	0.46	0.45
--------Publicly-Held Debt Attributable to Non-Social Security Policy--------									
1	48.35	29.74	27.01	96.25	74.16	71.12	47.9	44.4	44.1
5	45.39	29.65	27.34	87.26	68.61	66.07	41.9	39.0	38.7
10	44.76	30.48	28.49	80.07	62.10	59.62	35.3	31.6	31.1

Figure 1
Social Security Primary Surplus Share of GDP Under NRP and NRA ex PRAs*

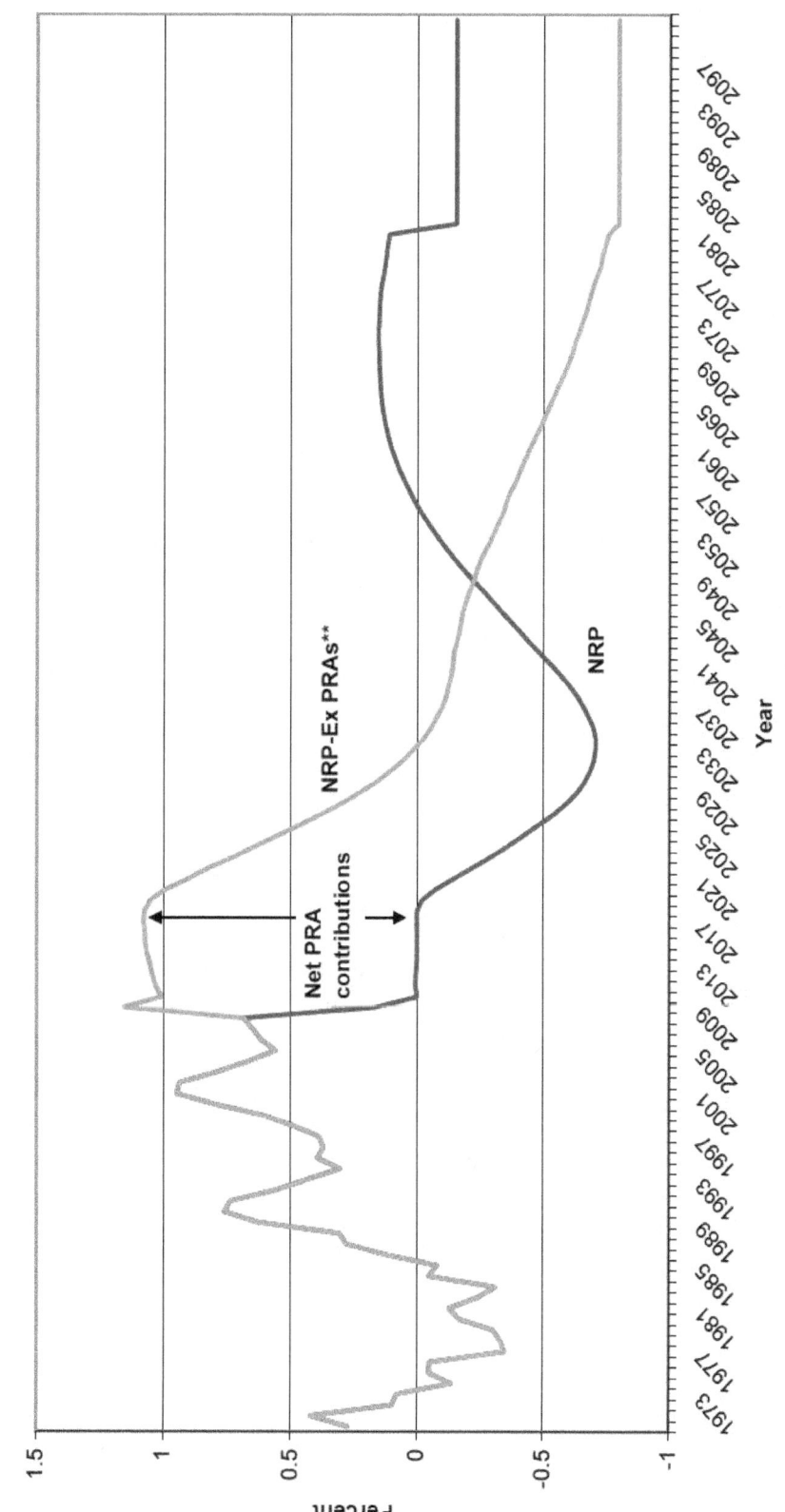

*NRP policy through 2080 as projected by Social Security actuary. After 2080, the net Social Security contribution share of GDP (including PRA net contributions) is assumed constant at the level that is consistent with both the Trust Fund and PRA balances as share of GDP being in steady-state. Total Social Security benefits and contributions (including PRA contributions and distributions) are the same under both policies, and Social Security's infinite horizon actuarial balance is precisely zero. To isolate the effect PRAs have on fiscal planning, PRAs are assumed to earn the same rate of return as the Trust Fund (imply no PRA administrative costs).

31

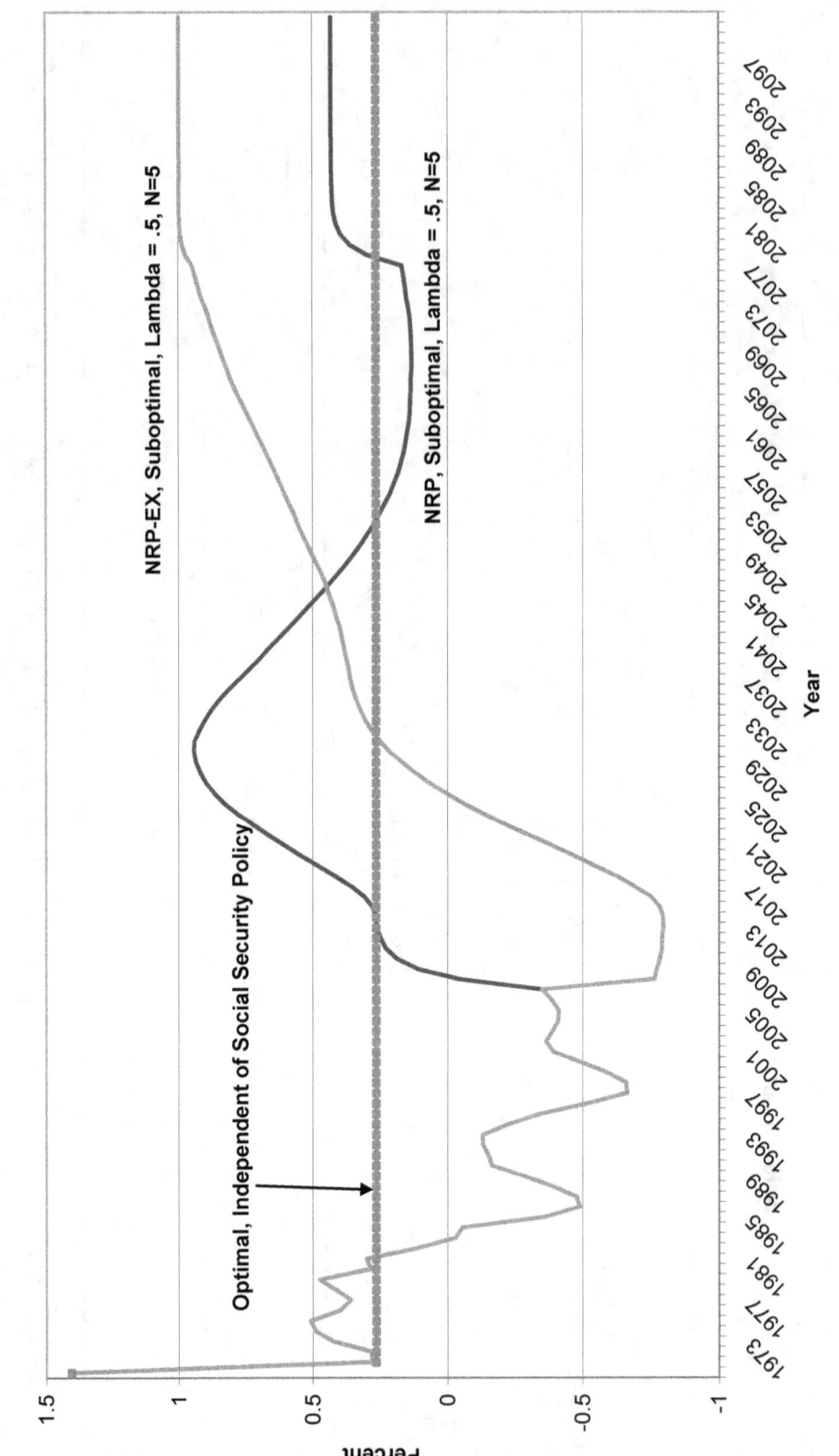

Figure 2
Simulated Non-Social Security Primary Surplus Share of GDP Starting
From 1969 Initial Conditions

NRP-EX, Suboptimal, Lambda = .5, N=5

NRP, Suboptimal, Lambda = .5, N=5

Optimal, Independent of Social Security Policy

Year

Percent

32

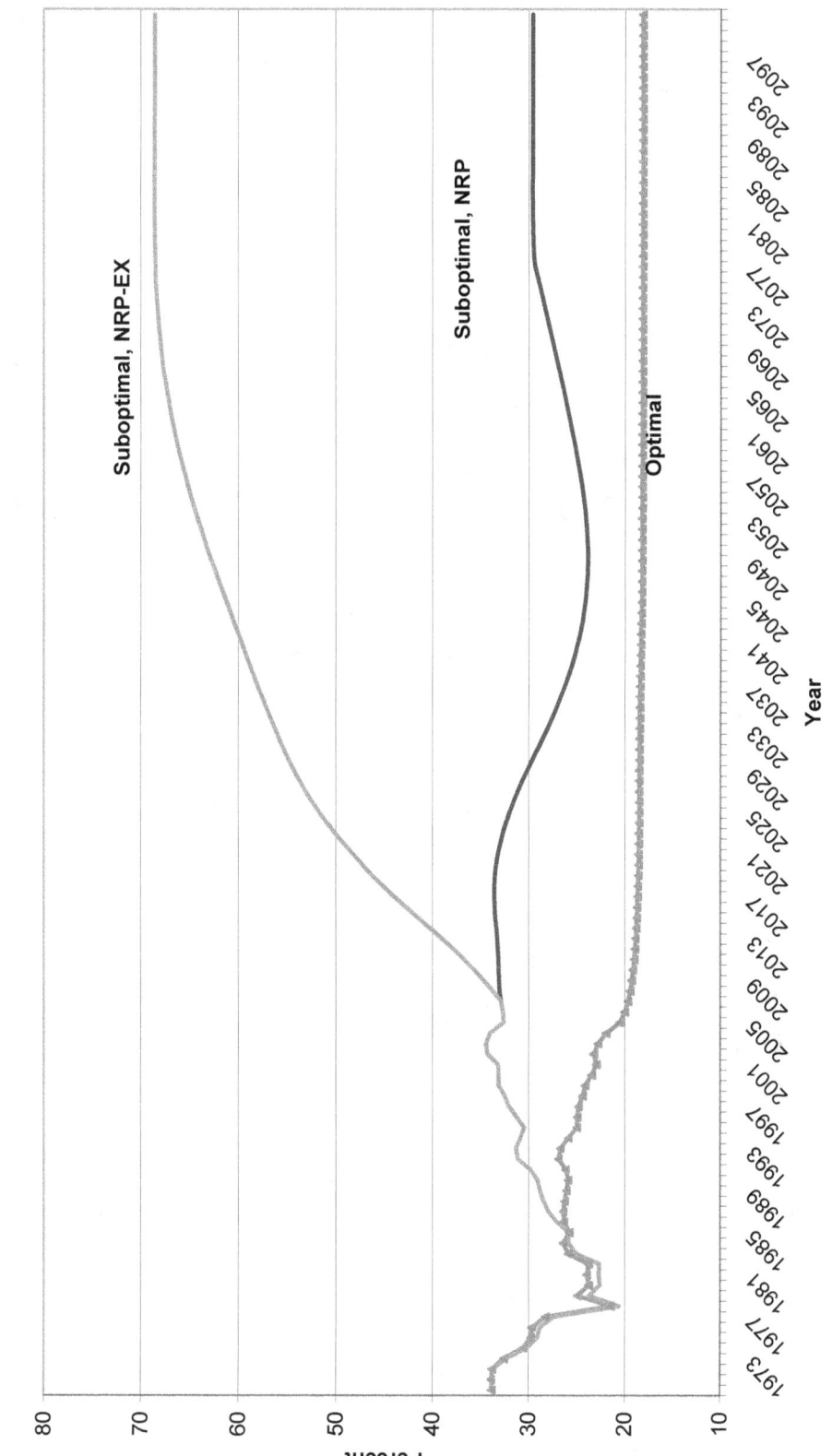

Figure 3
Simulated Time Path for Public Debt Attributable to Non-Social Security Policy
(Percent of GDP)

33

Figure 4
Simulated Time Path for Total Publicly-Held Debt
(Percent of GDP)

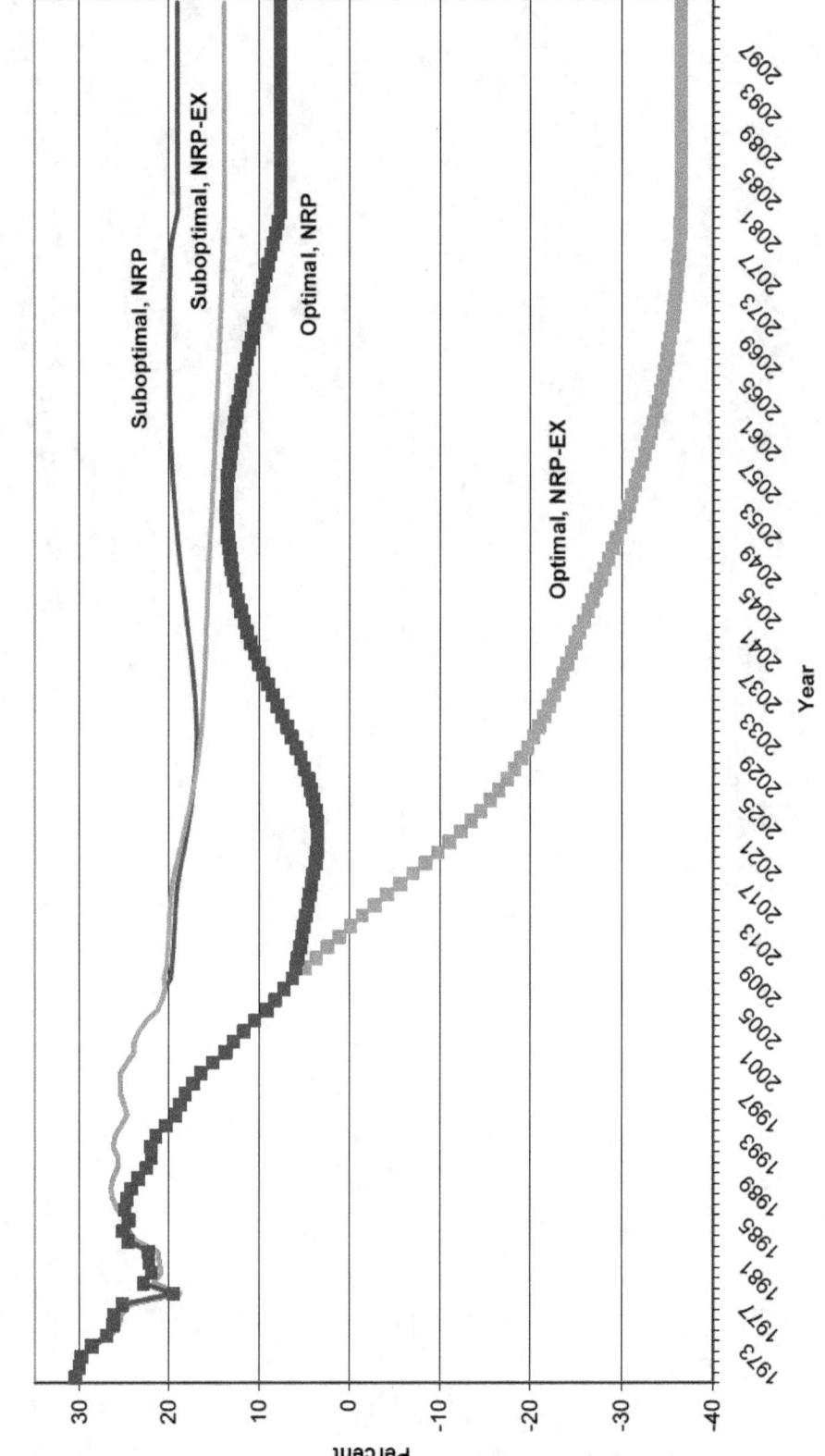

34

References

Blinder, Alan. 1990. "Political Effects of Social Security Surpluses, A Commentary." In Carolyn Weaver (ed.), *Social Security's Looming Surpluses, Prospects and Implications*, Washington D.C.: AEI Press.

Congressional Budget Office. 1999. Statement of Director Dan L. Crippen and Deputy Director Barry B. Anderson before the Committee on Ways and Means U.S. House of Representatives, February 23.

Congressional Budget Office. 2005. *The Long-Term Budget Outlook*, December.

Congressional Budget Office. 2007. *The Cyclically Adjusted and Standardized Budget Measures*. February.

Congressional Quarterly Weekly Report. 1997. "Social Security trust funds......at center of sound and fury." Vol. 55, Issue 5

Cutler, David, James Poterba, Louise Sheiner, and Lawrence Summers. 1990. "An Aging Society: Opportunity or Challenge?" Brookings Papers on Economic Activity. 1:pp.1-73.

Diamond, Peter and Peter Orszag. 2004. *Saving Social Security: A Balanced Approach.* Washington D.C.: Brookings Institution Press.

Elmendorf, Douglas W., Jeffrey B. Liebman and David W. Wilcox. 2001. "Fiscal Policy and Social Security Policy During the 1990s," Mimeo, July.

International Monetary Fund. 2005. "Staff Report for the 2005 Article IV Consultation with the United States of America" June 30.

Koitz, David; Geoffrey Kollmann and Dawn Nuschler. 2001. *Social Security and Medicare Lock Boxes*, Congressional Research Service Report RS20165, March 21.

Kotlikoff ,Laurence, Alan Auerbach, and Jagadeesh Gokhale. 1991. "Generational Accounts - A Meaningful Alternative to Deficit Accounting." In *Tax Policy and the Economy*, NBER vol. 5.

Liebman, Jeffrey, Maya MacGuineas, and Andrew Samwick. 2005. "Nonpartisan Social Security Reform Plan." December 14. (http://www.nonpartisanssplan.com/pages/1/index.htm)

Mariger, Randall. 1999. "Social Security Privatization: What Are the Issues?" National Tax Journal, December.

Mariger, Randall. 2008. "Do Social Security Surpluses Pay Down Publicly Held Debt? Evidence from Budget Data," mimeo, December.

National Economic Commission. 1989. Report to Congress and the President, March 1.

Novelli, Bill (with Boe Workman). 2006. *50+, Igniting a Revolution to Reinvent America,* New York: St. Martin's Press.

Office of Management and Budget (2002), FY2003 Federal Budget, Analytical Perspectives, Chapter 3.

President's Commission to Strengthen Social Security. 2001. *Interim Report.* August. (http://www.csss.gov/reports/Report-Interim.pdf)

Smetters, Kent. 2004. "Is the Social Security trust fund a Store of Value?" American Economic Review 94(2): 176-181.

Social Security Trustees. 2005. The 2005 OASDI Trustees Report. Washington D.C.: U.S. Social Security Administration.

Social Security Administration. 2005. Memorandum from Stephen C. Goss (Chief Actuary) and Alice H. Wade (Deputy Chief Actuary) to Jeffrey Liebman, Maya MacGuineas, and Andrew Samwick, "Estimated Financial Effects of 'A Nonpartisan Approach to Reforming Social Security'"
November 17. (http://www.ssa.gov/OACT/solvency/Liebman_20051117.pdf)

Social Security Administration. 2003. Memorandum from Stephen C. Goss (Chief Actuary) to Peter Diamond and Peter Orszag, "Estimates of Financial Effects for a Proposal to Restore Solvency to the Social Security Program." October. (http://www.ssa.gov/OACT/solvency)

U.S. Government Accountability Office. 2005. Statement of Comptroller General David M. Walker before the Committee on Ways and Means, House of Representatives. "Social Security Reform: Early Action Would Be Prudent." March 9.

Wildavsky, Arron and Naomi Caiden. 1997. *The New Politics of the Budgetary Process,* New York: Addison-Wesley.